Medieval Times

Author	Linda Milliken
Illustrator	Barb Lorseyedi

EP049 ©Highsmith® Inc. 1996, 2003, 2007
W5527 State Road 106, P.O. Box 800
Fort Atkinson, WI 53538

Table of Contents

The Hands-on Heritage series has been designed to help you bring culture to life in your classroom! Look for the "For the Teacher" headings to find information to help you prepare for activities. Simply block out these sections when reproducing pages for student use.

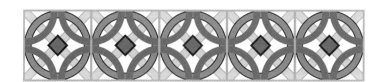

Medieval Times

Medieval times, also known historically as the Middle Ages, is the name given to the period in western Europe from the decline of the Holy Roman Empire, which began in A.D. 400, to the beginning of the Renaissance in A.D. 1500.

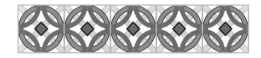

Churches and Cathedrals

The Christian church dominated the lives of people and provided leadership in the early Middle Ages. Popes, bishops, and other leaders of the church took over many functions of government after the Roman emperors lost power. The younger sons of noble families often entered the priesthood and were able to collect taxes, called *tithes*, from the villagers. The church also maintained courts of law.

Two church institutions, the cathedral and the monastery, became centers of learning. The monks of some monasteries and the clergy of the cathedrals helped maintain the reading and writing of Latin. They preserved many valuable ancient manuscripts and established most of the schools in Europe.

Lords and Manors

By the 800s, most of western Europe was divided into large estates called *manors*. Wealthy landowners, called *lords* or *noblemen*, ruled the manors, but most of the people were poor peasants who worked the land. Life was short and difficult. Most people never reached the age of 30. War, famine, and epidemics, such as the Black Death, killed many.

The Coming of Castles

After the end of Charlemagne's rule in 814, Europe was again divided into many kingdoms. Most of the kings were weak and had little control over their kingdoms. There was constant warfare. Homes became fortresses where inhabitants could defend themselves against the ongoing struggle for more land. These fortified homes, known as *castles,* were strategically built to provide protection for a lord and those who served him. A castle became the center of medieval life.

Medieval Times

Knights and Knighthood

The Age of the Knight began in about A.D. 900. New inventions such as the stirrup and horseshoe turned a horseman into a fighting force. Kings and lords needed knights for fighting. However, they could not maintain their cost in peacetime. So instead of paying wages, some kings and lords agreed to give portions of their land in exchange for services, mostly military. This arrangement of land for services was called *feudalism*. Any man granted land was called a *vassal*. A lord and a vassal had rights and duties toward each other. A lord promised his vassal protection and justice. Vassals tithed 10 percent of all goods to the lord. Vassals who became knights also arranged for lower class people, called peasants, to work their land.

In addition to working the fields, peasants protected and cared for livestock, cultivated new land, and worked in the vineyards and gardens of the lord. Peasants were very poor. Large families commonly lived together in one-room huts they shared with farm animals.

Growth of Towns

After the 1000s, many capable lords provided strong governments and periods of peace. Merchants again traveled the land routes. Towns sprang up along the main trade routes. Most early towns developed near a fortified castle, church, or monastery where merchants could stop for protection.

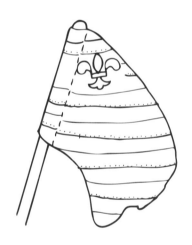

Peasants began to leave the fields and settle in towns. Here they sought work and developed crafts and the means to earn a living independent of the feudal system. Craftsmen banded together in groups called *guilds* to control their industry and maintain standards.

As merchants began to travel abroad, contact with the outside world increased. And so began the next historical period, the Renaissance.

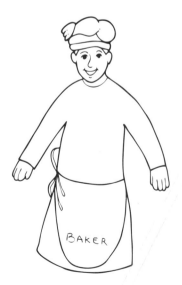

Names and Occupations

Many people in America can trace their last name back to a medieval trade or occupation. Often during the Middle Ages, a man came to be known by the name of his trade. A worker in metals was called a smith. If his name was John, he might come to be known around town as John, the smith. A pottery worker named David might be called David Potter. A man named James who was a fine hunter might be called James Hunter.

Many family names today have come from the trades of the Middle Ages. Such names as Carpenter, Miller, Baker, Weaver, Goldman, and Smith might well be traced to medieval craftsmen.

Castles

A castle was the home and fortress of a feudal lord. They were built to protect the nobleman's family and those who lived in or near them from thieves, rival lords, and invaders from other lands. Castle inhabitants included servants, soldiers, priests, tailors, and bakers who worked within the castle walls, as well as the peasants who tended the lord's farmland. The first castles were built from wood, but were later replaced by stone construction and surrounded by thick stone walls. There were round or square towers where the walls met. The main tower, with walls as thick as 9 feet (3 meters), was called the *keep*. It was here where the castle's lord, his family, and his knights ate and slept. There were several floors, each with a large fireplace and connected by a spiral staircase.

Toward the end of the Middle Ages, castles became very grand with more elaborate furnishings, window designs, and interior design.

Project

Construct a model of a castle.

Materials

- resource and picture books about castles
- Castle Building page
- cardboard
- construction paper
- milk cartons
- scissors
- yarn or string
- glue
- markers
- toothpicks
- student-supplied materials of choice

Directions

1. In cooperative groups, use the Castle Building page to help you create your castle.
2. Brainstorm ways to add detail to the castles. Remember to be creative in your use of materials and ideas while making the castle as authentic as possible. Use markers to draw stone walls or collect small stones to glue to the outside of walls and towers. Build toothpick ladders. Make toothpick and paper banners to fly from castle towers.

For the Teacher

Copy one Castle Building (page 6) per group. Provide each group with a large cardboard base.

Castle Building

Castle Keep and Towers

The lord and his family lived on several floors in the keep. There were other towers at each corner of the castle. There were holes in the thick tower walls to shoot arrows through.

Make a tower by cutting the top end off of a milk carton. Cover with construction paper. Cut arrow openings in the sides. Cut cardboard floors to add inside.

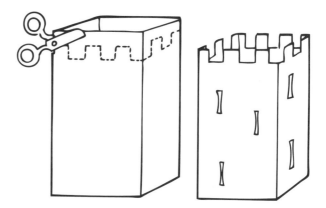

Castle Walls

The walls around the castle were very thick. Soldiers could stand on them.

Cut castle walls from cardboard. Notch the tops. Draw or glue stones.

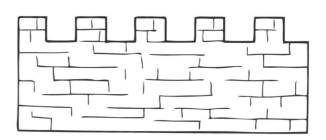

Inner Ward

The space in the center of the castle was called the inner ward. It was here that the business of the castle was carried out.

Create a scene that reflects castle life. Make miniature knights polishing their armor. Stack small boxes to resemble hay bales. Make a small cart with wagon wheels carrying a cargo of vegetables.

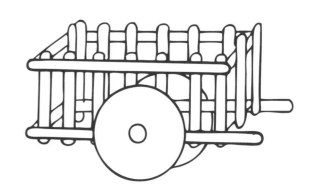

Gatehouse and Drawbridge

When a doorway was built in a wall it had a U-shaped opening and towers on each side. The opening was covered by an iron gate and led to a bridge that could be pulled up during an attack.

Cut an arch in the castle wall. Make two round towers and place one on each side. Criss-cross black construction paper to make a gate.

Cut a rectangular cardboard drawbridge and hang it at the gate with yarn.

Attack and Defend

Within the castle walls lived knights and soldiers who were ready to defend their lord's home. Every castle was stocked with provisions to last for several months. A *siege* (an attack by an enemy) could last that long and starving castle inhabitants was a common tactic. Attackers used a variety of giant *catapults,* wooden arms that hurled rocks over castle walls. Movable towers, called *siege towers,* enabled attackers to get to the top of castle walls. Battering rams were used to smash down the castle gate. Attackers set scaling ladders against, or tunneled beneath, the castle walls. Once inside the castle, the fighting was hand-to-hand with shields, crossbows, swords, mace clubs, and axes.

Castle defenders poured rocks and boiling oil or water on the attackers. Arrows were aimed through specially cut openings in castle walls. It wasn't until the 1400s that cannons became a popular form of defense and attack.

Project

Make and test a model of a medieval attack or defense method. Explain the purpose and evaluate its effectiveness.

Materials

- Attack and Defend Project Cards
- reference materials
- tall milk cartons
- craft sticks
- paper tubes
- cardboard, about 2 x 2 feet
- scissors
- string or twine
- construction paper
- student-supplied materials

For the Teacher

Decide whether students will work individually or in cooperative groups. Copy one Attack and Defend Project Card (page 8) for each student or group. Cut cards apart in advance.

Directions

1. Review the contents of your project card.
2. Select materials from the supply table or use other materials from home in order to complete your project.
3. Evaluate your results.

Attack and Defend Project Cards

Embrasure

An *embrasure* was an alcove in the castle wall, with a narrow opening to the outside which allowed defenders to shoot arrows without exposing themselves to enemies.

Cut an opening, as shown, in the cardboard. How far and accurately can you toss a pencil or wad of paper through the opening?

Battering Ram

A *battering ram* was a heavy beam of wood often with metal attached at the end. Men used it to ram walls, beating at the same spot, trying to make an opening.

Wrap the end of a wooden dowel or cardboard tube with a sock stuffed with newspaper. Place aluminum foil over the end.

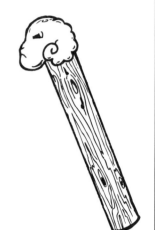

Siege Tower

The best way to get to the top of the castle wall was with a *siege tower*, a wooden shed, several stories high, set on rollers, with a drawbridge to span the top of the castle wall.

Use milk cartons and craft sticks to construct a siege tower. Can you propel toy soldiers over the top of a pile of books?

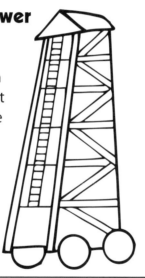

Trebuchet

A *trebuchet* had an arm up to 60 feet (18 meters) long and could sling giant stones up to 980 feet (300 meters).

Draw plans for the construction of a trebuchet. Include dimensions and projected trajectory. How heavy of an object do you think it could it throw and how far?

Catapult

The *catapult* had a wooden arm with a cup at one end that could fling rocks, flaming rags, dead animals, and other disease spreading materials.

Use cardboard, craft sticks, and twine to make a catapult. Test the distance you can propel objects such as marshmallows and small rocks. (Be safety conscious!)

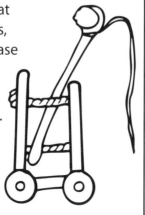

Siege Bow

Siege bows, or *ballistas*, were large mounted crossbows that shot huge arrows when the large bow arm was pulled back.

Cut a cardboard bow. Add a tight rope to each end. Cut a large cardboard arrow and test its shooting ability.

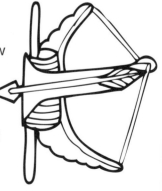

EP049 Medieval Times © Highsmith® Inc. 2007

Portcullis

The first defenses an enemy might encounter when attacking a medieval castle were a moat and a drawbridge. The second line of defense was a *portcullis*. The portcullis was a heavy wooden and iron grating that protected the entrance to a castle. It was made from criss-crossed bars of wood. The wooden bars were clad in iron to strengthen them. Spikes were formed at the bottom.

On the first floor of the castle tower, there was a room in which a gatekeeper stood guard. From here, the portcullis, connected by chains to a winch, could be lowered into position at a moment's notice.

Project

Construct a portcullis to use on a painting depicting life inside the castle walls.

Materials

- black and white construction paper
- tempera paint and brushes
- scissors
- glue

Directions

1. Paint a castle courtyard scene on white construction paper. You might show peasants at work or knights shining their armor. While the paint dries, make a portcullis.

2. Cut the length of black construction paper in to ½-inch-wide (1.27 cm) strips.

3. Overlap the strips to create a grid. Space the strips evenly apart, allowing at least ½ inch (1.27 cm) between them. Glue the grid together where the strips intersect.

4. Cut the bottom of each bar into a pointed shape to resemble a spike.

5. Glue the portcullis over the dry, painted scene. Cut the top into an arch.

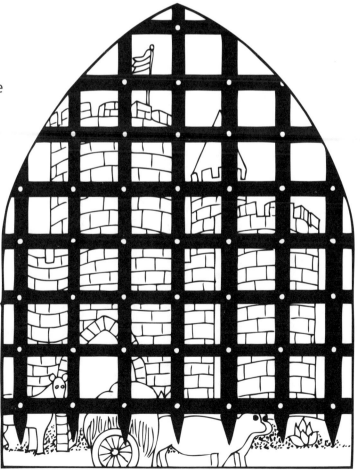

Great Hall

The great hall was the main room in a castle. It was used for eating, sleeping, and conducting business. It was often connected to the kitchen by a long passageway. In the evening, there were suppers and entertainment. It wasn't until the 1200s that the lord built extra rooms for himself and his family, away from the rest of the household.

It was in the great hall that feasts took place. Tables and benches—not chairs—were set up along the sides of the hall. A fire blazed in the center, and tapestries covered the stone walls. If royalty was present, a high table was placed at the end of the hall on a raised platform. The lord entertained with his finest gold goblets and plates.

For the Teacher

Project

Transform your classroom into a great hall for your medieval feast (see page 11).

Materials

- brown butcher paper
- white butcher paper
- napkins
- paper cups
- several small bowls
- salt
- plastic spoons

Directions

1. Move all the desks or tables end-to-end along two walls at opposite sides of the room. Arrange chairs on both sides. (Students will have to pretend they are sitting on benches!)

2. Place one table at the end of the two rows of desks, to form a U-shape.

3. Roll five to seven brown butcher paper logs. Stack them to "build a fire" in the center of the room.

4. Cover the tables with white butcher paper. Put a napkin, spoon, and cup at each seat.

5. Pour salt for into bowls and place them at intervals on the tables. Salt was generally sprinkled on food by all the guests.

EP049 Medieval Times © Highsmith® Inc. 2007

Medieval Feast

The lord and lady of a manor hosted great feasts in the castle hall. The food was plentiful and elegantly presented. Beef and mutton (sheep) were stewed with onions, garlic, and herbs. Venison (deer), swans, geese, and quail were roasted. A pastry, called a *coffin*, was filled with a mixture of meat, dates, ginger, vinegar, eggs, and herbs.

At royal meals, a peacock was cooked and reassembled with its feathers in place. Apples, pears, figs, grapes, oranges, and lemons were picked from the castle gardens. Cheese was made and butter was churned. Common vegetables were dried peas and beans. Cooks created spectacular desserts of sugar paste, marzipan, and jelly painted and molded into shapes like castles or ships. Milk was used chiefly for cooking such things as fine almond puddings.

Project

Use the ideas and recipes on this and the following three pages to plan and prepare a medieval feast. Choose a lord and lady to oversee the efforts. The rest of the class will be the serfs in charge of the preparations.

Materials

See individual recipes and preparation ideas.

Directions

1. Divide class into four cooperative groups. Assign three of the groups to be in charge of making something from the menu for the class.

2. Assign the fourth group the duty of preparing the great hall for the feast (see page 10).

3. Choose people to carry out the duties on the list found on page 12. Change jobs part of the way through the feast so that everyone has a chance to dine.

4. Select a king and queen to be seated at the royal table.

Medieval Feast

There were many duties that needed to be performed for a feast to take place. Look at the descriptions below and assign the duties to class members. They will be in charge of assembling the materials and carrying out the task. The materials needed, if any, are printed in bold.

Serfs

The serfs lived in huts provided for them on the lord's estate. In return, they were bound to serve the lord. When the time came for a royal feast, the serfs handled all the preparations and serving during the meal. They carried food from the kitchen, served trenchers, and scooped stew with a **ladle**. They offered fruit trays to the guests, cleared the trenchers, and served dessert.

Entertainers

The feast was not complete without entertainment for the diners while they ate. Minstrels played **musical instruments** and sang, jesters told amusing stories, and jugglers showed their skills with **juggling balls**.

Trumpeter and Drummer

The feast did not begin until the trumpeter announced the arrival of the king with fanfare from his **trumpet**. After the king was seated, the trumpeter again sounded his trumpet to indicate the start of the feast. The trumpeter blew his horn and the drummer beat on his **drum** between each food course.

Ewerer

There were no forks, but **napkins** were provided. Some food was eaten with spoons, but many people ate with their fingers. They used their little fingers to sprinkle **salt** from the **bowls** (*saltcellars*) to their food.

The Ewerer brought **a pitcher of water, a large bowl,** and **a towel** between courses so diners could wash their hands.

The Ewerer also tasted the water before pouring it over the king's hands.

Panter

The Panter had a very special assignment. He was the king's personal servant. He was in charge of seeing to the king's dining needs. The Panter carried special **trays** to bring food, trenchers, and saltcellars to the king.

EP049 Medieval Times © Highsmith® Inc. 2007

Medieval Feast

Fruit Platter

Materials
- plastic knives
- trays

Directions
Wash, dry, and slice oranges, apples, and pears. Arrange them on a tray around a cluster of grapes.

Beef Stew

Materials
- slow cooker
- 2 pounds stewing beef, cut in cubes
- 2 (8-ounce) jars beef gravy
- salt, pepper, crushed thyme, herbs of choice
- onions (optional)
- large spoon and ladle

Directions
Mix the beef and gravy in a slow cooker. Add seasonings and herbs to taste. Cut onions into thin wedges and add to stew mixture in slow cooker. (The addition of onions makes the recipe more authentic, but is optional depending on student tastes!) Cook on high for four hours or until meat is tender. *12 small servings*

Almond Pudding

Materials
- large mixing bowl
- 2 large packages instant vanilla pudding
- milk (check package for amount)
- almond extract
- hand mixer
- measuring cups and spoons

Directions
Prepare pudding according to package directions. Add a small spoonful almond extract. *16 small servings*

Bread Plates

The finest grains were grown at local manors, ground into flour at the lord's mill, and baked into bread in the castle kitchen or bakehouse. Some grains were used to bake *trenchers*—flat, coarse bread made from whole wheat.

Stale trenchers were used as dining plates. The trenchers soaked up the gravy from stews. The peasants ate their gravy-soaked trenchers, while the wealthy gave theirs to the poor or fed them to the dogs.

Project
Work in small groups to mix, roll, and bake trenchers to use as plates during a classroom medieval feast.

Materials
- 2 cups (480 ml) sifted all-purpose flour
- 3 tsp. (15 ml) baking powder
- 2 tsp. (2.5 ml) salt
- 4 cups (60 ml) shortening
- ¾ cup (180 ml) milk
- rolling pins and/or aluminum pie tins
- large bowl
- fork
- measuring cups
- aluminum foil
- oven

Directions
1. The recipe will make eight (8) trenchers. Work in groups this size to mix and make the trenchers. Each group will need the ingredients and materials listed.
2. Tear off a piece of aluminum foil for each student, large enough to roll the dough into a medium-sized plate.
3. Follow the baking directions.

Baking Directions
1. Combine the sifted flour, baking powder, and salt.
2. Use a fork to cut the shortening into the flour to make coarse crumbs.
3. Make a well in the dough and pour in the milk. Stir with a fork.
4. Divide the dough into eight equal pieces.
5. Knead the dough on the aluminum foil 12 times with the palm of the hand. Roll with a rolling pin or flatten with the bottom of a pie tin to about ½-inch (1.25-cm) thick.
6. Bake on the aluminum foil at 450 degrees for 12 minutes.

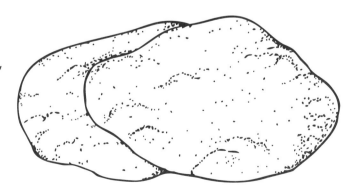

Pottery

Typical medieval pottery was often finished with a green glaze. Crude pottery jugs were used to carry ale or wine for the ordinary diners in the great hall. In order to make the jugs more attractive, potters often molded simple designs into the surface. A jug's base might be just a flat surface, or it may have a foot trim. Spouts were generally of two types: a "pinched" spout was achieved by squeezing or pinching the jug's rim; a "tubular" spout was formed by attaching a hollow tube to the jug. A jug's contents were poured into equally crude mugs.

Eventually jugs were made from copper alloy. It was still characteristic, however, for the jugs to feature simple designs.

Project
Make a pottery jug or mug.

Materials
- self-hardening clay
- green paint
- paintbrushes
- clear lacquer spray
- toothpicks, for engraving

Directions
1. Choose whether you would like to shape a mug or jug from the clay.
2. Use toothpicks to engrave the sculpted piece.
3. Paint the mug or jug green after the clay has hardened.
4. Spray with clear lacquer.

Medieval Towns

With the revival of trade, people who had lived on a manor and had developed a skill wanted to become more independent. They wanted a chance to pursue economic opportunities that towns provided. Usually a group of tradesmen built a settlement outside the walls of a castle, along the crossroads of a trade route. Medieval towns tended to be small because walls were built around them for protection as they grew. Most buildings were constructed of wood. Since homes were also heated with wood and lighted by candles, fires were a major and constant concern.

Tradesmen and craftsmen each had their own sections within a town. People engaging in the same craft usually located on the same street, with the street being named according to the craft—Tailor Street, Tanners' Row, and so on. When people went out at night they carried torches on the dark streets

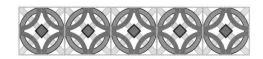

For the Teacher

Project

Form cooperative groups to paint a mural depicting a street scene in a medieval town.

Materials

- butcher paper cut to size for a mural
- pencils
- paint
- glue
- construction paper
- scissors
- sketching pencils
- reference materials

Directions

1. Review the Cobblestone and Medieval Towns pages for more information on medieval streets and homes. Ask each group to make a list of what they might include in their mural.

2. Have students sketch a street scene on the butcher paper. Paint the final scene. Cut and glue construction paper detail to add dimension such as flags and cobblestone.

EP049 Medieval Times © Highsmith® Inc. 2007

Cobblestone

Since space was limited in medieval towns, houses were crowded together and were usually built two or three stories high. Streets were narrow, winding, unpaved, and often filled with pigs, horses, and rubbish. People disposed of their garbage and human waste by simply dumping it into the street. So disease spread easily and quickly.

During the 1200s, rough cobblestones became a common way for townspeople to "pave" their streets. These rounded stones were simply laid over the dirt streets. Although the uneven surface was difficult to walk on, it was far better and more sanitary than before.

Project

Recreate a cobblestone pattern.

Materials

- shoebox lid
- rubber cement
- stones and rocks
- small toy car or truck or toy with wheels
- small objects such as erasers, paper clips, etc.

Directions

1. Gather some rocks and stones. Select the ones that are smooth and somewhat flat.

2. Try to pave the box lid with stones. How difficult is it to get an even surface and keep the stones close together?

3. Pile several things on top of your toy truck (erasers, paper clips, etc.). Push or pull the vehicle along your homemade cobblestones. What happens? Discuss what difficulties cobblestones may have presented for people in medieval times.

Marketplace

Several times a year, usually around a religious holiday, a town might hold a giant fair to which merchants came from distant places to sell their wares. During this time, tumblers and minstrels, as well as trained bears and horses, would perform their tricks. During the rest of the year, markets were held in the town square one or two days each week for people from nearby manors.

Everyday life was quite different. The shops of craftsmen lined the streets. The shops were similar to booths with shutters that opened during market hours. Here, on the first floor of their home, the craftsmen were busy at work and offered their items for sale. Hanging over the shop doors were signs with painted pictures suggesting the business of the shop owner—a boot for the cobbler, a ring for the goldsmith, bread for the baker, and so on.

Project

Design and make a shop owner's sign.

Materials

- 11 x 17-inch sheet of white construction paper
- paint stirrer (available at paint stores)
- paint
- paintbrushes
- scissors
- glue

Directions

1. Decide on a profession or craft to depict on a sign.
2. Determine an object or picture that would symbolize that craft or profession.
3. Sketch the object vertically on the construction paper, leaving a two-inch (5.08-cm) margin at the top and bottom. Cut the top and bottom margins as shown in the illustration.
4. Paint the final sketch.
5. Paint the paint stirrer a corresponding color. Glue the banner to the paint stick.

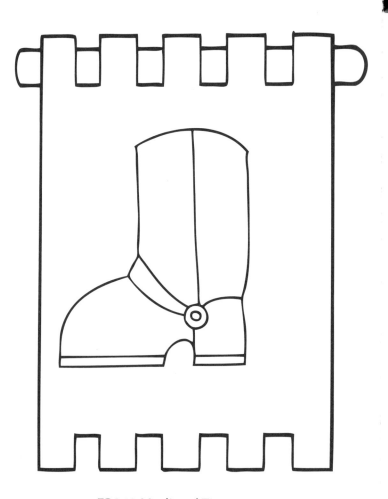

EP049 Medieval Times © Highsmith® Inc. 2007

Knights and Knighthood

A young boy of noble birth who would later train to become a knight spent the first years of his life with his family learning to ride a pony and care for horses. At age seven, he became a *page* in another noble-man's household where he learned to hunt, play chess, and practice chivalrous behavior. He also served meals to castle diners. At age 14, he became a squire. He trained for battle and the joust and performed important castle tasks such as pouring the wine or carving the meat. He acted as a personal servant to a knight. He was responsible for taking care of the knight's armor, war horse, and weapons. If neces-sary, the squire accompanied the knight to battle. At 21, when training was complete, he was knighted in a ceremony called the *accolade*. Dressed in a white shirt, gold tunic, and purple cloak, a squire knelt before the man knighting him, who tapped him with a sword on each shoulder and stated, "Be thou a knight." After the 1100s, this distinction also brought with it independence and a parcel of land.

Project
Make a four-part accordion-fold picture showing the progressive steps to becoming a knight. Conduct a knighting ceremony and award *Knight of the Realm* certificates.

Materials
- 2 large sheets white construction paper
- crayons
- clear tape

Directions
1. Fold each piece of construction paper in half, widthwise.
2. Tape them together end-to-end making an accordion-fold at the tape connection.
3. Illustrate a step toward knighthood on each page—early boyhood, page, squire, knight

For the Teacher

Knighting Ceremony
1. Copy one knighthood certificate (page 20) per student
2. Cut a cardboard sword in the shape shown below.

3. Have students wear white. Place a purple cape around their shoulders, and touch them on each shoulder with the sword. State the words of knighthood, "Be thou a knight." Present each knight with a certificate.

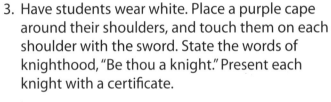

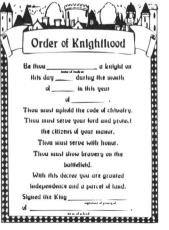

Order of Knighthood

Be thou _____ a knight
name

on this _____ day during the month

of _____ in this year

of _____.

Thou must uphold the code of chivalry.

Thou must serve your lord and protect
the citizens of your manor.

Thou must serve with honor.

Thou must show bravery on the battlefield.

With this decree you are granted
independence and a parcel of land.

Signed the Ruler _____
signature of principal

of_____.
name of school

EP049 Medieval Times © Highsmith® Inc. 2007

Armor

In the late Middle Ages, a knight wore a full metal bodysuit, called *plate armor,* for protection in combat or displays of skill. Because the outcome of a battle depended not only on the skill of the knight but also on the strength of his armor, *armorers* (makers of armor) became respected craft workers.

A knight was dressed in armor by his squire, who always worked from the feet up. The last thing to go on was the helmet. While a helmet usually weighed between 3 to 7 pounds (1½ to 3 kg), some weighed over 16 pounds (7.4 kg). It was strapped to the body armor, so the knight's shoulders bore the incredible weight. The helmet had a visor that opened like a door. In the 1500s, it was fashionable to decorate the visors on helmets worn at tournaments. A knight's helmet had a crest of feathers or other light material.

Project
Make a knight's helmet to wear at a tournament.

Materials
- black construction paper or tagboard
- pencil
- large sheet construction paper, color of choice
- 2 metal brads
- scissors
- stapler
- glue
- Helmet Pattern

Directions
1. Cut out the pattern pieces.
2. Fold sheets of black construction paper or tagboard in half.
3. Place the pattern's dotted lines on the fold of paper and trace. Cut out along the outline without cutting the fold.
4. Assemble the helmet as shown in the illustrations at right. Use the rectangle-shaped pattern for size extension.
5. Use metal brads to attach the visor to the helmet at points A and B.
6. Cut a large feather from the colored paper. Staple it to helmet.

For the Teacher
Copy one Helmet Pattern (pages 22–24) per student.

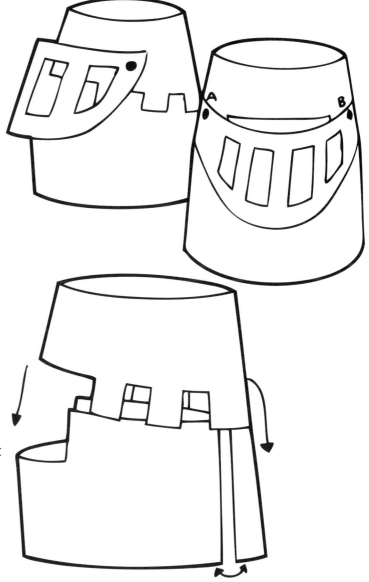

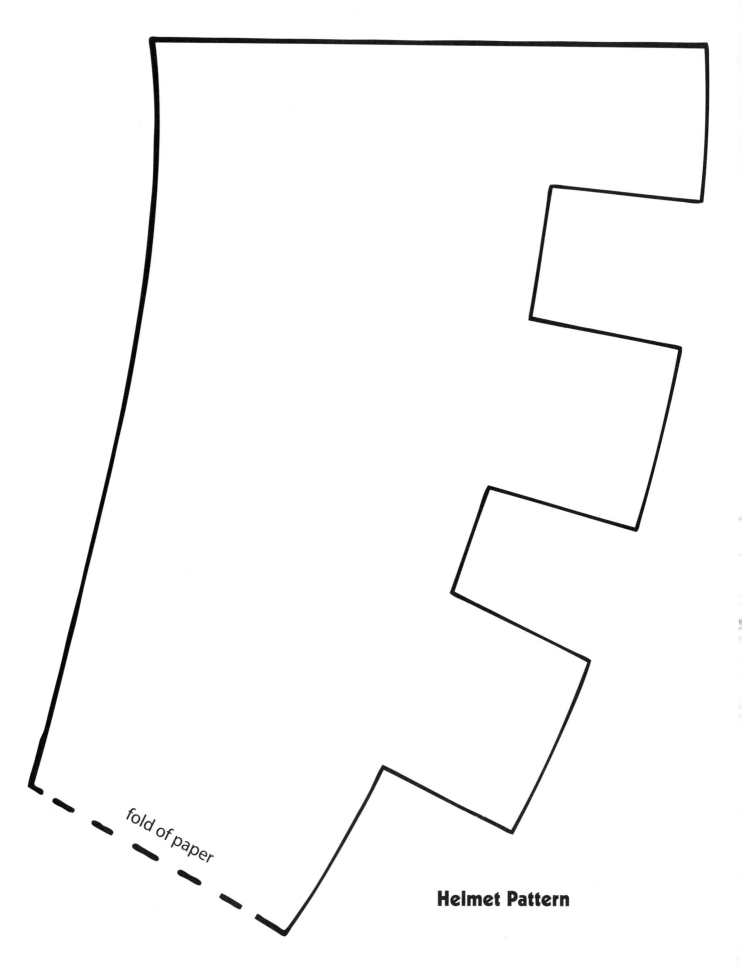

fold of paper

Helmet Pattern

EP049 Medieval Times © Highsmith® Inc. 2007

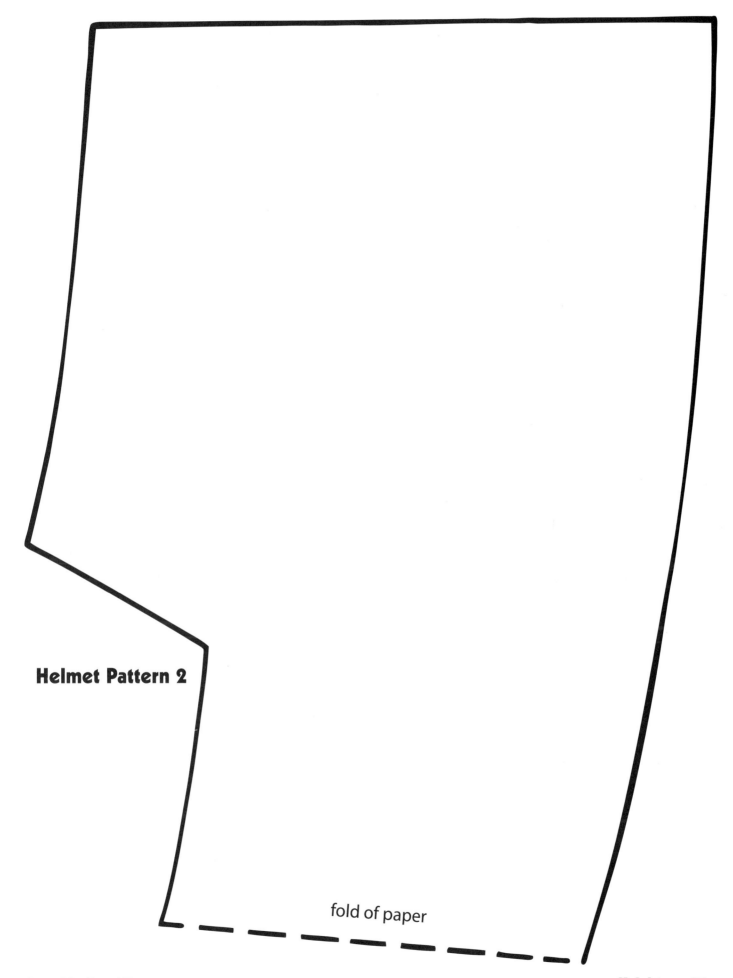

Helmet Pattern 2

fold of paper

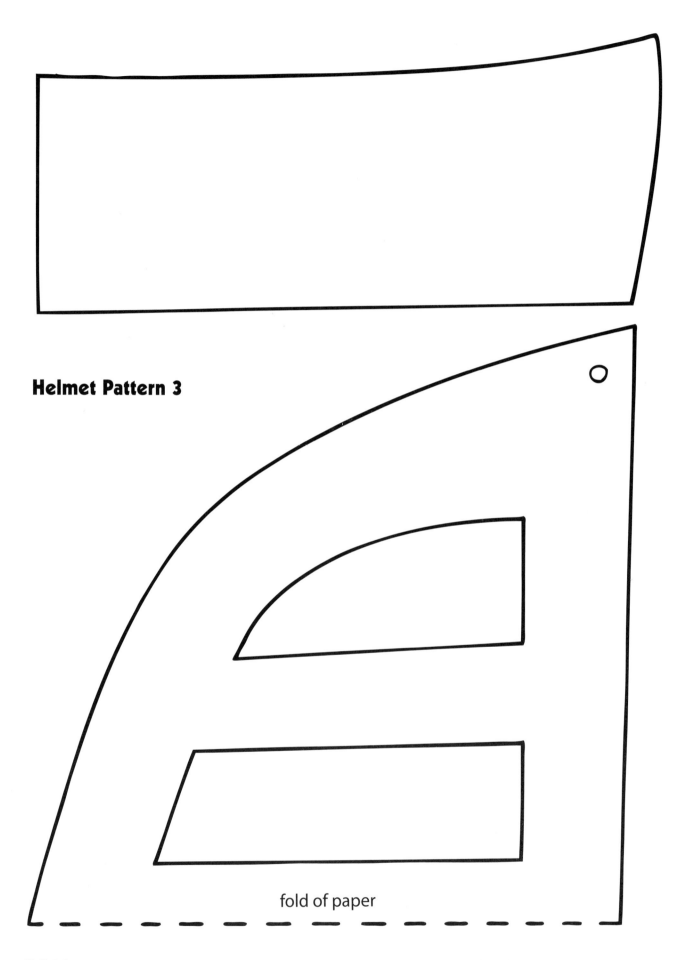

Helmet Pattern 3

fold of paper

EP049 Medieval Times © Highsmith® Inc. 2007

Tournament

Knights practiced their skills during peacetime by competing against each other in mock battles called *tournaments*. These "battles," waged over the whole countryside and lasting all day, provided training for wartime. The defeated knights usually had to pay a hefty ransom—items of considerable value such as horses, armor, and weapons—to the victors.

These free-for-alls were eventually replaced by the one-on-one competition known as the *joust*. These events were organized spectacles with colorful banners flying from the grandstands. Ladies, dressed in their finery, sat in the gallery among the other spectators, and there was also a seat of honor for the "Queen of Love and Beauty." Sometimes a knight wore a "favor," a scarf or handkerchief belonging to a lady who favored him. If he won his event, he presented the "favor" to his lady tied on his lance.

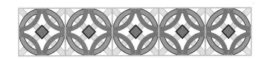

For the Teacher

Project

Plan a "tournament" with games and other activities drawn from medieval life.

Materials

The materials needed, as well as playing and scoring rules, are listed under each activity on page 26.

Directions

1. Choose two students to be judges and to keep score. Choose a female student to be the Queen of Love and Beauty, who will watch the competition from a seat of honor (a chair decorated with crepe paper streamers).

2. Divide the rest of the class into two teams. Have each team select colors and design and paint a butcher paper banner for the team and a cardboard shield for each participant.

3. Make jousting lances (page 28).

4. The judges may select the games and events to be staged and determine their scoring rules and order of competition.

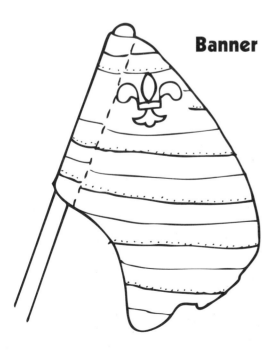

Banner

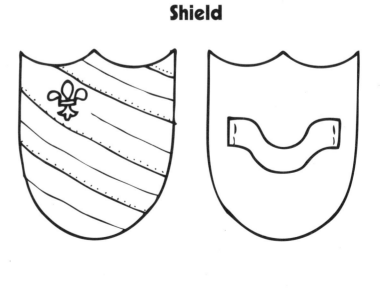

Shield

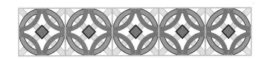

Tournament Activities

Ball Toss

A common medieval game was playing catch with a ball made of leather or cloth, stuffed with almost anything! Sometimes the ball was hit over a net or raised mound of earth with a gloved hand.

Have each team stand on opposite sides of a net. Toss a beanbag or small ball back and forth. If a team fails to make the catch, a point is scored for the opposition.

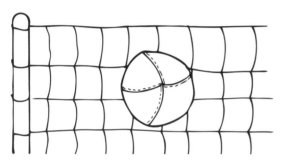

Quintain

A quintain was similar to a crossbar with a shield on one side and a weight on the other. It was used for lance practice. The squire had to hit the shield on the crossbar and duck before the sandbag on the other end swung around and hit him.

A player from an opposing team gently tosses a beanbag at a competitor. The competitor tries to block the throw with his/her shield. Score one point for a blocked throw and one point for a throw that hits a player. Allow three throws per competitive pair.

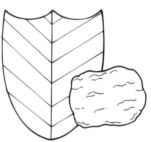

Armor Race

A squire attended the tournament to assist his knight by carrying his banner and helping him put on his many layers of armor.

Have a relay race. Gather an identical number and type of clothing for each team. Form pairs within each team. At the judges' command, one pair from each team works to dress one of them in armor (the layers of clothing). At the judges' approval, the clothes are removed and the next pair repeats the steps. The first team to have all its pairs finish is declared the winner.

Lance Accuracy

It was important for a knight to be accurate with the thrust of his lance. In battle, it was a matter of life or death!

Hang a plastic ring from the end of a stick. Secure the stick to the crossbars of the swings or monkey bars.

Each player, in turn, charges at the ring, lance drawn! As the ring is approached, the player tries to put his or her lance through the ring, letting go of the lance as the pass is made. If the lance goes through the ring a point is scored.

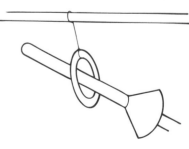

EP049 Medieval Times © Highsmith® Inc. 2007

Chivalry

Chivalry was the complex set of codes and ideals that guided a knight's life. The code included a devotion to duty, fair play on the battlefield, honesty, good manners, and bravery. A knight was expected to protect the weak and the poor and show respect toward women. He was to be generous and courteous to all. He fought against injustice and evil and faced any enemy with valor. Above all, a knight defended the church and was ready to die for it. A knight who was found guilty of cowardice or other misconduct faced public shame. He was stripped of his armor, his shield, his spurs, and his sword.

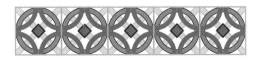

Project
Cooperatively, write a code of chivalry for your classroom. Conduct "round table" discussions in which chivalrous acts are shared and acknowledged.

Materials
- butcher paper
- markers
- masking tape

Directions
1. Tape a large sheet of butcher paper to the wall.
2. Select a scribe (secretary) to record all information.
3. Write "Code of Chivalry" across the top.
4. As a class, create a list of rules, based on medieval standards of chivalry, to govern behavior inside and outside your classroom.
5. Hold weekly round table discussions to evaluate the effectiveness of the code and to honor chivalrous conduct.

Jousting

Jousting was a contest between two knights on horseback that tested their horsemanship and weapons skills. The knights charged at each other on horseback with heavy, blunt lances and shields and tried to knock each other to the ground. Both wore armor and their horses were covered in embroidered cloth. The wooden lances splintered easily on impact.

A joust could also be a form of "trial by combat" in which a man accused of a crime might prove his innocence in victory. Several jousts comprised a tournament and the victorious knight was often granted great honors and prizes.

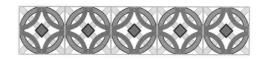

Project
Make a safe, lightweight jousting lance for use in tournament games.

Materials
- paper tubing from gift wrap or paper towels
- wide tape
- crepe paper (optional)
- construction paper
- tempera paint and brushes

Directions
1. If you have paper tubing from rolls of gift wrap, the length is satisfactory. If you are using paper towel tubing, tape several together end-to-end to achieve the desired length.

2. Paint the paper tubing to match the chosen colors of the tournament teams. Wrap the tubing with crepe paper to make candy cane stripes (optional).

3. Make a cone from a half-sheet of construction paper. The smaller opening should be able to slide over the paper tube. Secure the cone in place about eight inches (20.32 cm) from one end.

4. Pinch the tube closed at the opposite end.

For the Teacher
See page 25 for Tournament Games.

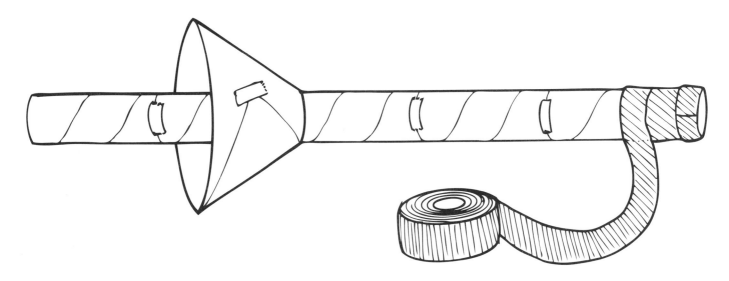

Brass Portraits

Cathedrals and churches of the medieval period sometimes contained detailed engravings of knights in armor. The portraits were usually made to honor an exemplary and famous knight who had died. The completed portraits were set in gravestones on the church floor or on top of raised tombs.

Skilled tradesmen carefully engraved these portraits onto a sheet of metal very similar to brass, showing accurate detail in their engravings. They were able to engrave each link in the knight's mesh mail, shield details, and armor designs. Paint was sometimes applied to add color to the knight's flag or shield.

Project
Engrave a detailed portrat of a knight.

Materials
- cardboard rectangle approximately 12 x 6 inches (30.48 x 15.24 cm)
- toothpicks
- aluminum foil
- permanent colored markers
- clear tape
- drawing paper, pencil

Directions
1. Cover the cardboard with aluminum foil. Tape the edges to the back side of the cardboard.
2. Sketch a knight on drawing paper cut to the same size as the cardboard.
3. Lay the drawing over the foil-covered cardboard. Use a toothpick to trace over the drawing. Press hard, but not so hard as to tear the paper.
4. Lift off the drawing paper. Use the toothpick again to carefully retrace any lines that did not imprint clearly.
5. Color portions of the engraving with permanent markers.

For the Teacher
Cut enough cardboard pieces in the appropriate size in advance for each student.

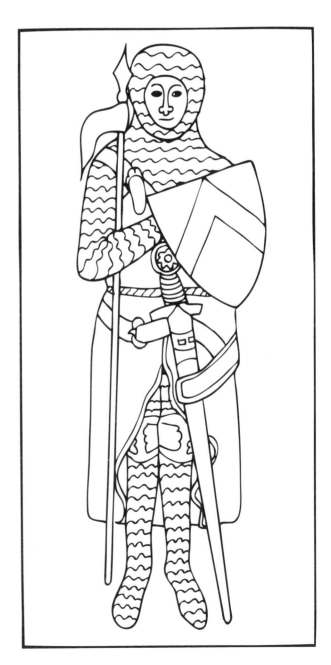

Gems and Jewels

Women of medieval western Europe liked to display their rank by wearing rings and brooches. These pieces of jewelry were usually fashioned from gold, with precious stones set among engraved designs of human figures and coiled monsters. Some took the shape of animals that were also represented on the family's coat of arms. Wearing the brooch showed allegiance to the family.

During the latter part of the Middle Ages, jewels were also used to adorn hats and belts. Jewels encrusted the crowns of royalty and headwear of noble women.

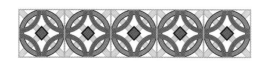

Project
Design and make a jeweled brooch.

Materials
- pin backs
- recycled costume jewelry, beads, sequins
- hot glue or tacky glue
- cardboard or poster board
- gold or other paint, brushes
- puffy paint (optional)
- tissue paper in a variety of colors

Directions
1. Cut a cardboard shape for the brooch. The shape should be wider or longer than the pin backing. Review the illustrations for ideas.
2. Paint the cardboard backing. While gold is preferred, any color selection is fine.
3. When the paint has dried, glue "jewels" to the cardboard shape. If costume jewelry is not available to take apart, roll tissue paper wads in bead shapes or use puffy paints to create dimension.
4. Glue the pin backing to the cardboard.

For the Teacher
Pin backs are available in bead or hobby shops.

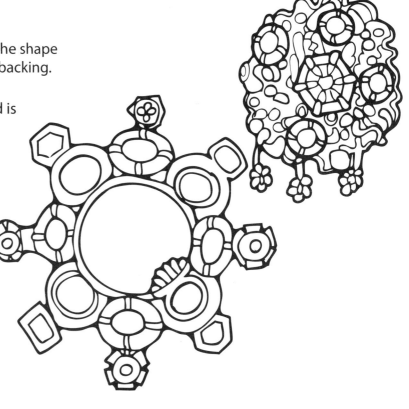

Seals and Signets

During the Middle Ages, people of all classes, noblemen included, often could not read or write. Instead of signing a document, they added a wax seal pressed from a metal die. The seal was sometimes incorporated into a smaller design called a *signet* and engraved into a ring. The signet ring was practical as well as decorative. The wearer simply turned his hand over and pressed his signet ring into the waiting hot wax.

The engraving in the seal often reflected a family's heraldic design. Occasionally they included initials. Military leaders attached their seals to military orders. Seals were also used in dies for badges and medallions.

Project

Carve a die from foam to make an individualized signet ring for printing on medallions and classroom documents.

Materials

- foam meat trays
- toothpicks
- modeling clay
- pipe cleaners

Directions

1. Cut the foam tray into 1-inch circles.
2. Use toothpicks to engrave a design into the foam.
3. Poke two holes through the foam and thread a pipe cleaner through the holes.
4. Twist the pipe cleaner to fit your index finger.
5. Practice pressing the signet into modeling clay.

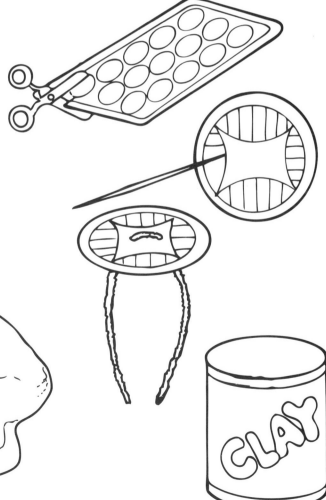

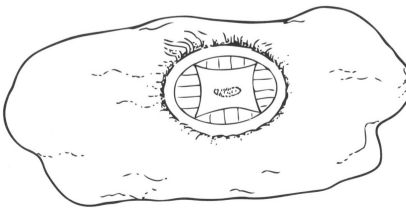

Coat of Arms

Heraldic designs were important during medieval times and were found in many aspects of life. The suit of armor made it difficult to distinguish friend from foe on the battlefield, so it was a natural choice for knights to choose symbols as their marks of identification. Each knight had his own heraldic design marked on his shield, his tunic, and even on the cloth covering his horse. This design was known as a *coat of arms.*

Most people during the Middle Ages did not know how to write. In order to prove the authenticity of documents, it was common to use a seal with a person's heraldic design as a signature or a way to identify a particular family. The design commemorated an event, occupation, or outstanding quality in one's life. A *herald* was selected to supervise the selection of colors and symbols so there would be no duplicates.

Project

Design a family coat of arms to paint on a shield.

Materials

- Shield Pattern
- large sheet colored construction paper
- drawing paper
- crayons
- tempera paint
- paintbrushes
- scissors

Directions

1. Create a heraldic design for a personal coat of arms. Begin by sketching and coloring a first draft of the design. Be sure the design symbolizes an interest or event in your life. Submit the design to the classroom "herald" for review.

2. After the design has been reviewed and approved, paint it in the shield pattern.

3. Cut out the shield when the paint has dried.

4. Glue the completed shield to contrasting construction paper.

For the Teacher

Copy one Shield Pattern (page 33) per student. Select a "herald" to review the design for duplicates and approve the final design.

Shield Pattern

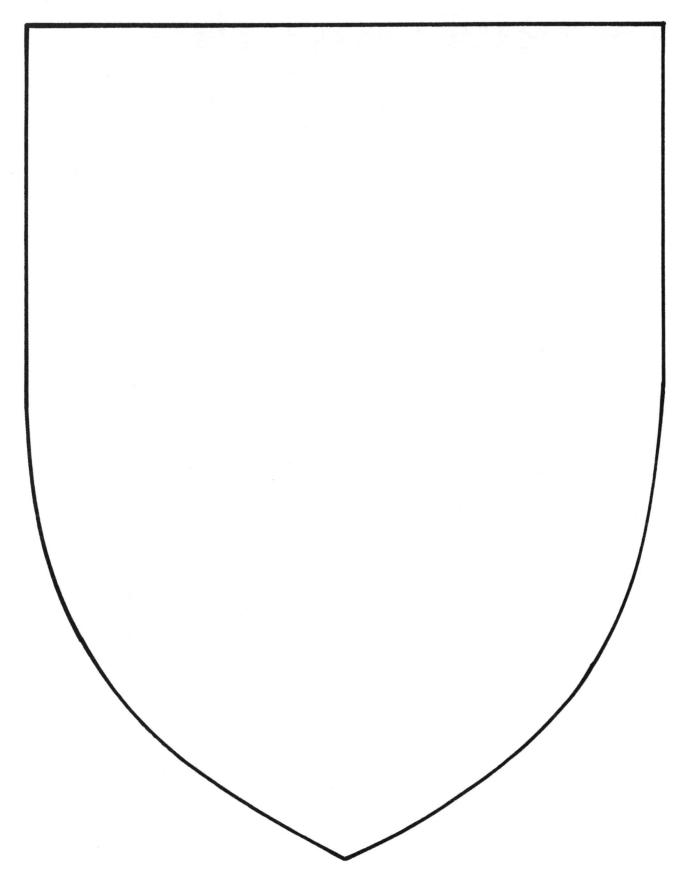

Manuscripts

During the Middle Ages, manuscripts were written on a high-quality parchment called *vellum*. Monks worked in a special place in the monastery called the *scriptorium* and produced most of the books.

Manuscript production was highly specialized. While one group of monks prepared the vellum, another group did the writing. The third group became involved by decorating the manuscripts. A fourth and final group of monks was responsible for placing the finished manuscripts in the library, selling them, or trading them to other monasteries.

The majority of books produced during the Middle Ages were Bibles or other religious books. Nonreligious topics included books about beasts, called *bestiaries*, romances, and writings of ancient Greek and Roman authors.

Project
Form cooperative groups of four to six members to produce a manuscript complete with illuminations and binding.

Materials
- white typing paper or other lightweight paper
- crayons, watercolors, or markers
- black ink pens
- hole puncher
- shoelace or yarn

Directions
1. Work together to write a *bestiary*—a tale about an imaginary or legendary medieval beast. Divide that tale into equal parts, one for each group member.

2. Each member rewrites his or her part of the story with black ink on white typing paper.

3. Work individually or in pairs to decorate (illuminate) each page.

4. Select two members of the group to bind the manuscript by placing the pages in order, punching holes along one edge, and "stitching" them together with a shoelace or yarn.

5. Select two more members to read the manuscript to the rest of the class.

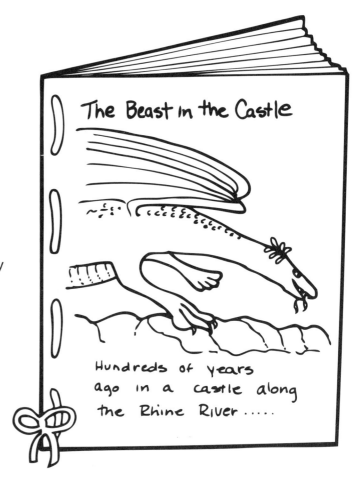

EP049 Medieval Times © Highsmith® Inc. 2007

Illuminations

The Middle Ages provided many manuscripts that were decorated with beautiful pictures and designs in a variety of colors. Gold or silver leaf was often used on the initial letters and for decoration. The pictures, designs, and decorations on a manuscript page were called *illuminations*, because the bright and gilded colors of the manuscripts appeared illuminated. Different styles of illumination developed throughout Europe. However, six basic forms were used in all: animals, branches with leaves or berries, ornamental letters, geometric designs, braids, and scrollwork.

Some illuminators were monks, while others were professional painters, both women and men. Their miniature pictures added interest and were helpful in telling the story.

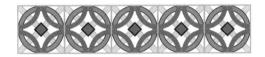

Project
Create an "illumination" in the form of an ornamental alphabet letter.

Materials
- half-sheet white construction paper
- paint, markers, and/or crayons
- gold and silver ink pens

Directions
1. Sketch the outline of the first letter of your last name in a large block letter on the construction paper. Outline the letter in dark crayon.
2. Paint or color a design inside the outline.
3. Use gold or silver ink pens or a combination of the two to add detail inside the letter.
4. Decorate with crayons and pens around the letter.

Troubadours

People of the Middle Ages were great lovers of poetry and legends. As they could not read, storytellers or recitalists of verses, were very popular. Wandering poet-musicians, known as *troubadours*, traveled through the land entertaining lords and ladies with tales of love, chivalrous deeds, and the bravery of knights.

Many castles had troubadours of their own who resided there and entertained guests after dinner. The troubadour accompanied himself on the lute or perhaps a harp. Recitals of romantic tales and lengthy poems about a favorite hero were especially popular. King Arthur and his Knights of the Round Table, Robin Hood of Sherwood Forest, and Saint George and the Dragon were particularly favorite subjects.

Project

Videotape an oral presentation based on a troubadour's talents—tell a story, recite a poem, or sing a song about medieval people and life.

Materials

- video camera
- literature selections featuring legends about dragons and knights
- musical instruments such as an autoharp, drums, recorder, or stringed instruments

Directions

1. Form cooperative pairs. Together, find or write a legend, poem, or song about medieval times.
2. Practice your presentations. One presents the material, the other accompanies on a musical instrument.
3. Videotape the presentations.

Clothing

The clothing worn by the men and women of the early Middle Ages varied according to their social standing. A peasant's dress was very simple, while a nobleman's attire was elaborate, especially the sleeves of the garment. A knight wore a sleeved undertunic of linen or wool, reaching below the knees. Over this was a sleeveless tunic, called a *surcoat*, open at the sides and fastened with a belt. It was covered with a coat of arms. Men wore loose breeches or long stockings under their tunics. The woman's tunic developed into a long dress with oversized armholes and worn over a long-sleeved gown. Cloaks were often worn over the tunics.

Clothes for the wealthy became more colorful in the 1300s. Dozens of buttons decorated the outer garments. The surcoat was often edged with fur. The sleeves buttoned tightly from wrist to elbow. Jeweled felt hats and capes lined in fur were popular. Shoes became so pointed that the fronts were curled up and fastened to knees with small jeweled chains.

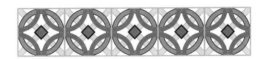

Project

Make a decorated surcoat for boys and girls.

Materials

- old pillowcase
- scissors
- turtleneck shirt or T-shirt
- leather belt
- fabric markers or paints
- buttons
- fake fur (optional)
- needle and thread
- glue

Directions

1. Cut two armholes and a neck hole from the sides and closed end of a pillowcase.

2. Draw or paint a design or crest on the front. Stitch or glue buttons and/or fur trim.

3. Wear the surcoat over a turtleneck or T-shirt. Wear a leather belt around the waist.

Headwear

Throughout medieval times, hats were often worn to indicate social status. Head coverings worn by the lower classes, as they toiled in the fields, provided much needed protection from the sun. Kings and church officials wore headwear to indicate their position of authority. And, of course, knights wore armor to protect their heads in combat.

During the 1100s and 1200s, women wore metal hair nets and veils. Draped throat covers, called *wimples,* were worn with various hood-like coverings. Men wore hoods that had long tails called *liripipes*. By the 1300s, people began to wear hats for decoration, resulting in a large variety of hat styles. Eastern influences resulted in hats that resembled turbans. During the 1400s, many European women wore a tall cone-shaped hat with a streaming veil called a *hennin*.

Project

Design a medieval head covering.

Materials

- Medieval Headwear page
- assorted fabrics
- trims such as fur, sequins, and lace
- pliable wire
- white glue and tacky glue
- stapler
- construction paper
- scissors
- illustrated books about medieval times

Directions

1. Review the Medieval Headwear page, as well as any other resources available.
2. Create a hat or form of headwear based on the pictures and information gathered from materials of choice.

For the Teacher

Copy one Medieval Headwear (page 39) per student. Provide additional resources if available.

As an extended activity, students may assume the identity of a person who might have worn the hat and share an aspect of his/her medieval life.

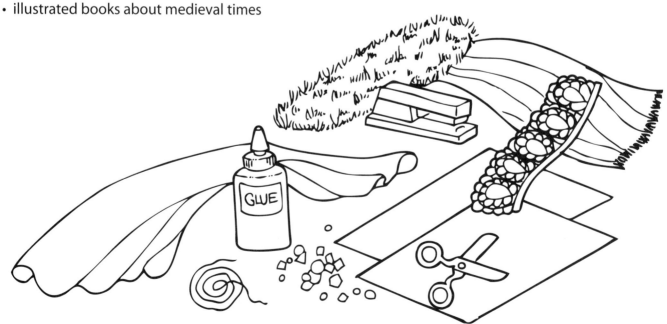

EP049 Medieval Times © Highsmith® Inc. 2007

Medieval Headwear

Troubadour

This hat of cloth with a rolled band and sometimes a long tail was worn by troubadours, jesters, and other entertainers.

Ladies in Waiting

Attendants to the lady of the manor wore a cloth draped over their head and held in place with a rolled fabric band. Embroidery and jewels were sometimes added.

Noble Woman

Jewel-encrusted metal hair nets were fashioned to fit over the top and sides of the head.

Noble Woman

A cone-shaped hat called a *hennin* was worn during the 1400s. It measured from 3 to 4 feet (0.9 to 1.2 meters) high and had a long, flowing veil.

Villein

The hard-working villeins (peasants and castle servants) protected their heads with draped fabric or caps.

Lord and Lady

Decorative fabric hats were rolled and stacked to resemble turbans. Fur, jewels, and lace-like trims were added for further decoration.

Page

A boy of noble birth, training to become a knight, wore a hat similar to an upside-down bowl.

King and Queen

A royal crown was worn as a symbol of supreme authority. This circular headwear was usually made of gold, engraved and ornamented with precious gems.

Games

People of all classes gathered in the great hall of the castle for meals and entertainment. Board games such as checkers and backgammon were popular among all people. Children played a board game called "Fox and Geese." Chess was a favorite because it had a mock battlefield where players could develop strategy and pieces could attack each other. Marbles and horseshoes were other popular activities. Adults even played children's games such as "Blindman's Bluff."

Boys' games taught them how to behave like knights. One game was called "Robber" and another "The King Doesn't Lie." Boys also made hobbyhorses and showed off for girls by charging at each other.

For the Teacher
Project
Learn to play one or more of the popular medieval games.

Materials
- checkers and checkerboard
- backgammon board
- marbles
- chess board
- horseshoes
- carpet squares

Directions
1. Set up an area in the classroom where board games can be played. If there is room, set several carpet squares on the floor and establish an area for marbles.

2. Pair one student who knows how to play a game with one who doesn't. Discuss and implement peer-group teaching with the students.

3. Invite students to create their own rules for games such as "Robber" and "The King Doesn't Lie." Have them think about how a medieval child might have played the same game.

Dragons

Dragons are mythical creatures found throughout stories and legends of ancient and medieval times. Legends describe them as large, lizard-like creatures that breathe fire and have long, scaly tails. Some people who lived during the Middle Ages blamed fire-breathing dragons for the destruction of crops, cities, and other calamities. Dragons were also blamed for stealing jewels from the wealthy and cattle from nearby farms. According to medieval legends, dragons lived in wild, remote regions of the world and guarded stolen treasures in their dens. It was believed that a person who killed a dragon gained its wealth.

The dragon was also a popular heraldic symbol, found on shields and family crests.

Project
Combine the popular medieval art technique of pen and ink with crayon resist to paint a dragon.

Materials
- black ink pens or thin black markers
- white construction paper
- colored construction paper
- watercolor paints and brushes
- crayons
- scissors
- glue

Directions
1. Use a black pen to draw a picture of a dragon.
2. Color the picture heavily with crayon between the pen lines.
3. Paint a watercolor wash, the color of choice, over the entire paper.
4. When dry, cut out the dragon and glue it to a contrasting color construction paper.
5. As an extended activity, relate the dragon to a literature selection or write a new legend about a dragon that lived during medieval times.

Gargoyles

The construction of a cathedral sometimes extended over as many as two or three centuries. One generation planned it and another finished the work. Lofty windows were filled with stained glass of exquisite colors. The Gothic arches of doorways and ceilings were ornamented with figures of saints and angels. The tops of pillars were carved with lace-like foliage.

On the edges of the roofs, stonecutters placed stone figures of creatures. Through the mouths of these figures, rainwater drained from the roof. These carvings were called *gargoyles*, which means gullet (throat). They received their name because of the gurgling noise the water made when passing through them. It was not unusual for gargoyles to project as much as 3 feet (91 cm) from the building. Originally intended to protect the building from the effects of rain, the gargoyles also became an important decoration on medieval cathedrals.

Project

Create a milk carton gargoyle. Practice pouring water through its spout.

Materials

- small milk carton, washed and dried
- construction paper
- tissue paper
- aluminum foil
- clear tape
- paper cup, water
- sink or plastic tub

Directions

1. Lay carton on its side as shown. Open the milk carton spout. Cut a hole in the backside of the milk carton.

2. Use a combination of aluminum foil, tissue paper, and construction paper to wrap the milk carton and create a gargoyle. Remember that a gargoyle was grotesque in appearance.

3. When the gargoyle is complete, pour water through the top and let it drain through the open spout. Make sure you do this over a sink or plastic tub. Discuss the purpose of the drainage.

For the Teacher

Students may refer to historical pictures of medieval cathedrals to create more authentic gargoyles or they may create original designs based on information gained above.

Cut hole here

Relics

Relics were skeletal remains or possessions esteemed and venerated because of association with a saint or martyr, and they were worshipped by people throughout medieval Europe. People felt that possessing or touching a relic might heal illness or help them obtain entry to heaven. A new cathedral offered a resting place for the sacred remains of knights and religious clergy. Elaborate sanctuaries were constructed within the cathedral to house the most revered relics.

Christians made pilgrimages to well-known shrines. They would wear a symbolic badge to represent the pilgrimage. There was also a vast business in the trading of relics.

Project

Work in pairs to design an elaborate box to house the relic of a medieval figure.

Materials

- boxes of all sizes
- scissors
- paint, paintbrushes
- macaroni noodles
- trims and fake jewels

Directions

1. Working in pairs, decorate a box to become the "shrine" for a medieval relic.

2. Find a "relic" to place inside the box. Conduct some research prior to selecting a relic and be prepared to explain its historical significance. For example:

   - a piece of metal: "This is from the armor of Sir Galahad, a famous Knight of the Round Table."

   - a bone: "This is part of the skeleton of Charlemagne, a great ruler who united many kingdoms during the eighth century."

   - a piece of cloth: "This is a piece of fabric from the cloak worn by St. Francis of Assisi before he gave up worldly possessions."

May Day

Of all of the holidays, May Day, a merry celebration of the arrival of spring, was the most important for the poor people during the Middle Ages, particularly those in England. Long before daybreak, peasants headed into the woods to gather and cover themselves in newly-bloomed flowers. They adorned every door and window with fresh boughs, garlands, and nosegays.

The greatest treasure of the day was the Maypole brought back from the woods by several yoke of oxen, with a nosegay of flowers tied to the tip of each horn. The huge pole was raised, decorated with flowers, and wrapped with colorful streamers from top to bottom. A banner flew from the top. Villagers seized the streamers and danced around the Maypole. There were archery contests and games. The winner was crowned with a laurel wreath.

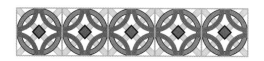

Project
Make a garland of flowers to decorate classroom walls and doors.

For the Teacher
Hang students' floral garlands around the classroom.

Materials
- tissue paper in assorted colors
- green crepe paper
- scissors
- thin wire or clear tape
- green construction paper

Directions
1. Accordion-fold squares of tissue paper. Wrap thin wire or tape tightly around the center. Fluff the edges to create flowers.
2. Twist lengths of green crepe paper to resemble vines and stems. Tape the flowers to the crepe paper. Add construction paper leaves.

EP049 Medieval Times © Highsmith® Inc. 2007

Guilds

During the later Middle Ages, town craftsmen formed associations called *guilds* according to the kind of work they did. There were guilds of carpenters, weavers, millers, butchers, bakers, grocers, tailors, goldsmiths, shoemakers, and so on. No one was allowed to engage in a craft unless he was a guild member. Officers were chosen, dues were levied, and honesty in trade was promoted and monitored. A guild helped its members by caring for its sick and poor.

Important guilds had their own halls in which guild business was conducted. Each guild had a banner on which the emblem, showing the tools of their craft, and their motto were displayed. Guild members had uniforms, called livery, which they wore during meetings. The livery was usually of two colors, scarlet and green, black, or deep blue.

For the Teacher

Project

Form cooperative groups to make a guild livery, a uniform representing a medieval craft.

Materials

- butcher paper
- scissors
- yarn
- crayons or tempera paint
- stapler
- paintbrushes

Directions

1. Divide into groups of four. Have each group select a different medieval craft to represent.

2. Have each member cut butcher paper "aprons" (see illustration). Staple yarn to tie around the neck and waist.

3. Have the group members design an emblem and motto for their craft. (Reference the guild banners shown below.)

4. Paint or color the guild design and write the motto on the apron. Hold group presentations with members wearing their guild livery that describes the medieval craft.

   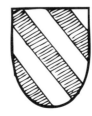 

| Wheelmakers | Hatters | Candlemakers | Painters | Bakers |

Metalwork

Metals of various kinds were combined for many practical uses during the Middle Ages. A metalworker (or smith) worked to forge horseshoes, harnesses, and stirrups. An armorer created the metal armor worn by knights. Nails of all sizes were everyday necessities. A metalworker also made thimbles for the seamstress and tools for the laborer. Lead was poured into molds to create figurines, plaques, and badges. Individually cast keys locked everything from chests and caskets to castles. Castles had other metalwork needs, including elaborate door hinges and barrel hoops. A heavy iron gate, called a *portcullis*, protected the castle entrance.

Project
Design elaborate hinges for a medieval door.

Materials
- aluminum foil
- half-sheet brown construction paper
- scissors
- glue

Directions
1. Round the top of the construction paper to form an arched door.
2. Cut aluminum foil into elaborate shapes.
3. Glue the shapes to the door to resemble hinges.

Literature List

Crispin, at the Edge of the World
by Avi. Hyperion, 2006. 262 p. Gr. 3–6
The companion to Avi's Newbery Medal winner, *Crispin, the Cross of Lead*, about an orphaned peasant boy in fourteenth–century England.

How to be a Medieval Knight
by Fiona Macdonald. National Geographic Society, 2005. 32 p. Gr. 2–5
Colorful illustrations and brief text cover the job requirements of a medieval knight in a question-and-answer format.

In the Time of Knights: The Real-life Story of History's Greatest Knight (I Was There Book)
by Shelley Tanaka. Hyperion, 2000. 48 p. Gr. 4–7
A fictionalized account of William Marshall, twelfth century knight. Well–illustrated with photographs, period reproductions and documents, and Greg Ruhl's illustrations. A fascinating glimpse into this time period.

Marco Polo and the Silk Road to China
by Michael Burgan. Compass Point Books, 2002. 48 p. Gr. 3–6
A biography of the thirteenth–century Venetian explorer whose book about his travels across Asia and work for Kubla Khan helped to launch the Age of Exploration.

Matilda Bone
by Karen Cushman. Clarion Books, 2000. 176 p. Gr. 5–6
Fourteen-year-old Matilda, an apprentice bonesetter and practitioner of medicine in a village in medieval England, tries to reconcile the various aspects of her life, both spiritual and practical.

The Medieval World
by Rebecca Stefoff. Benchmark Books, 2005. 48 p. Gr. 4–8
Overview of the history and culture of Europe during the Middle Ages.

Medieval World: Children and Games in the Middle Ages
by Lynne Elliott. Crabtree Publishing, 2004. 32 p. Gr. 4–8
One of a series of 20 titles that explores the daily lives of people living in western Europe between A.D. 500 and A.D. 1500. Includes time lines, maps, illustrations, and artwork from medieval manuscripts.

Merlin and the Making of the King
retold by Margaret Hodges. Holiday House, 2004. 39 p. Gr. 3–6
Hodges retells four Arthurian legends, "The Sword in the Stone," "Excalibur," "The Lady of the Lake," and "The Last Great Battle."

Ms. Frizzle's Adventures: Medieval Castle
by Joanna Cole. Scholastic, 2003. 40 p. Gr. 3–6
Don't miss this large-format adventure with Ms. Frizzle and company.

The Puppeteer's Apprentice
by D. Anne Love. Margaret K. McElderry, 2003. 186 p. Gr. 3–6
Set in medieval England, this accessible story is about a young orphan known as Mouse who follows her dream of becoming a puppeteer's apprentice.

The Travels of Benjamin of Tudela: Through Three Continents in the Twelfth Century
by Uri Shulevitz. Farrar, Straus, and Giroux, 2005. 48 p. Gr. 3–6
A fictionalized account of the travels of Benjamin, a Jewish man from Tudela, Spain, who, in 1159, set out on a 14-year-long journey that took him to Italy, Greece, Palestine, Persia, China, Egypt, and Sicily.

Whittington
by Alan Armstrong. Random House, 2005. 191 p. Gr. 4–6
Whittington, a feline descendant of Dick Whittington's famous cat of English folklore, appears at a rundown barnyard and restores harmony while telling his ancestor's story. Newbery Honor book.

Glossary

accolade—ceremony in which a man was given his knighthood

armor—a complete bodysuit made of metal that was worn by knights as protection

battering ram—heavy wooden beam used to ram castle walls and gates during a siege

bestiary—a book of stories about animals or beasts

castle—fortified home; a lord would turn his home into a fortress to protect himself and those who served him

catapult—a huge wooden arm with a cup at one end used to fling large stones and other objects during a battle

chivalry—the code, rules, and values that guided a knight's way of living

coat of arms—an emblem or symbol used to identify the members of a family; the design usually represented some aspect of the family's beliefs or history

embrasure—an alcove in a castle wall with an opening to the outside through which arrows could be shot

feudalism—system where a king gave land to a knight in exchange for the knight's services

gargoyle—stone carving on a medieval cathedral roof that served as a water spout to drain rain. It was usually in the shape of a strange creature

guild—an organization formed by people who worked in the same trade; the guild watched over the quality of work done and protected and helped its members

herald—official in charge of overseeing the designs of coats of arms; it was his responsibility to see that there were no duplicates

illumination—colorful hand-painted decorations on the pages of some medieval books; the designs sometimes included gold or silver

joust—a contest of warfare skills between two knights on horseback

knight—a man raised to special military rank and pledged to chivalrous conduct

lord—wealthy landowner who ran an estate

manor—large estate or section of land

portcullis—a heavy wood and iron grating that protected the entrance to a castle

relic—skeletal remains or an object worshipped because of its association with a saint or a martyr

scriptorium—the part of a monastary where the monks worked on copying and illuminating books

siege—a prolonged attack by an enemy

siege bow—a large mounted crossbow used in battles; also called a ballista

siege tower—a wooden shed that was several stories high which could be rolled up to a castle wall; from there, fighters could go over the wall on a drawbridge

tithe—tax collected by the medieval Church

trebuchet—a giant sling that was used to throw rocks over a castle wall during battle

trencher—flat piece of bread that was used as a plate to absorb gravy

troubadour—poet, musician, or storyteller who traveled from castle to castle to provide entertainment

vassal—a man who was granted land under the feudal system

vellum—a form of parchment made from animal skin; most of the books of medieval times were written on vellum